Wake Tech. Libraries
9101 Fayetteville Road
Raleigh, North Carolina 27603-5696

Y0-CJF-480

Mysterious Encounters

The Afterlife

Rachel Lynette

KIDHAVEN PRESS
An imprint of Thomson Gale, a part of The Thomson Corporation

THOMSON
GALE

Detroit • New York • San Francisco • New Haven, Conn. • Waterville, Maine • London

© 2008 Thomson Gale, a part of The Thomson Corporation.

Thomson and Star Logo are trademarks and Gale and KidHaven Press are registered trademarks used herein under license.

For more information, contact
KidHaven Press
27500 Drake Rd.
Farmington Hills, MI 48331-3535
Or you can visit our Internet site at http://www.gale.com

ALL RIGHTS RESERVED.
No part of this work covered by the copyright hereon may be reproduced or used in any form or by any means—graphic, electronic, or mechanical, including photocopying, recording, taping, Web distribution or information storage retrieval systems—without the written permission of the publisher.

Every effort has been made to trace the owners of copyrighted material.

LIBRARY OF CONGRESS CATALOGING-IN-PUBLICATION DATA

Lynette, Rachel.
  The afterlife / by Rachel Lynette.
     p. cm. -- (Mysterious encounters)
  Includes bibliographical references and index.
  ISBN 978-0-7377-3642-7 (hardcover)
  1. Near-death experiences--Juvenile literature. 2. Future life--Juvenile literature. I. Title.
  BF1045.N4L96 2007
  133.901'3--dc22

2007021478

ISBN-10: 0-7377-3642-9

Printed in the United States of America

Contents

Chapter 1
The Near-Death Experience   4

Chapter 2
Children and Near-Death Experiences   15

Chapter 3
Accidents and Near-Death Experiences   24

Chapter 4
Medicine and Near-Death Experiences   33

Notes   40
Glossary   42
For Further Exploration   44
Index   46
Picture Credits   48
About the Author   48

Chapter 1

The Near-Death Experience

What happens after we die?" People have been asking this question throughout history. Many people turn to religion for the answer. Religions like Christianity and Islam teach that every person has a **soul** that lives on after the body dies. What a person does during his or her life determines if he or she goes to heaven to be with God or to the fires of hell. Many people who follow Eastern religions, such as Buddhism or Hinduism,

Opposite: An illustration of a person having a near-death experience.

> ## Drugs and NDEs
> **The drug ketamine has been shown to produce NDE-like experiences in some of the people who use it. These people report feeling as if they were dead and having many of the common near-death experiences such as leaving the body, traveling down a dark tunnel, and communicating with God.**

believe in **reincarnation**. They believe that people live many lives and that how a person behaves in one life determines who or what they come back as in the next life. For example, a man who is rich but selfish and cruel might be reincarnated as a poor man in his next life. Still other people believe that nothing happens after death. For them, there is no soul, and the afterlife does not exist.

No matter what people believe, most agree that the only way to know exactly what happens after death is to die. Most people who die stay dead, and so they cannot tell those who are still living what the afterlife is like. But sometimes people die, or come very close to dying, and then come back to life. Some of these people say that they encountered the afterlife while they were "dead." These people have had what researchers call a **near-death experience** (NDE). People who have had NDEs are sure that there is an afterlife because they believe that they have experienced it. More than 13 million people in the United States have claimed to have had NDEs.

What Is an NDE Like?

People who have had NDEs often have difficulty describing them. They say the experience was so intense and so unlike anything they have ever experienced that they cannot describe it in words. People say things such as, "There are just no words to express what I am trying to say."[1]

Almost everyone who has had an NDE has sensed leaving their body.

Every NDE is unique; however, people who study NDEs have found that there are some common elements that NDEs share. No NDE will have all of the elements, but all NDEs have at least some of them. Researchers have also found that the longer a person was dead, the more intense and complete their NDE is likely to be.

Almost all people who have an NDE have a sense of leaving their physical bodies. Some people actually experience a sensation of floating or of being pulled out of their bodies. Often a person rises several feet above his or her body and then watches the scene below. Remarkably, many people who have had this experience have reported seeing and hearing things that they could not have known about had they not been in the room watching. For example, a person may be able to describe with complete accuracy the doctors and nurses and what they did and said.

Once they realize that they have died, most people are not upset about it. Often they are overcome with feelings of great happiness and well-being. If they were in pain before they died, they no longer feel it.

Another common element is traveling through a dark space, often described as a tunnel, toward a bright light. Most feel that it is important to get to the light at the end.

At the end of the tunnel most people find that they are bathed in a brilliant light. Some people find themselves in a pleasant place, such as a beautiful garden.

> ## NDEs Unprovable
> **NDEs cannot be proved by science because only the person having the NDE actually experiences it. This means that the NDE is not observable by other people and therefore cannot be verified.**

Often people meet spiritual beings in the light. These beings might be friends or family members who have died, angels, spiritual guides, Jesus, or God. Usually, the beings radiate light and love and seem to be there to help the people. Often the people feel an overwhelming sense of joy and bliss.

Adults sometimes experience what researchers call a **life review**. During this experience people see their whole lives pass before them. During life reviews people see both the good and bad things they have done and how their actions have affected other people. Sometimes people are given glimpses into their futures or shown things about how the universe works.

Sometimes the people are given a choice: either to remain in the afterlife or to go back to their previous lives. Often there is some sort of a barrier, such as a doorway, a bridge, or a pool of light. The people know that if they go through this barrier they cannot go back to their earthly life. In many cases they are commanded to go back because it is not yet their time to die. Some people travel back through the tunnel, others just suddenly find themselves back in their bodies, conscious and alive.

Who Has NDEs?

Anyone who dies or comes very close to death can have an NDE. The way the person dies does not

Anyone who actually dies or comes close to death can have an NDE.

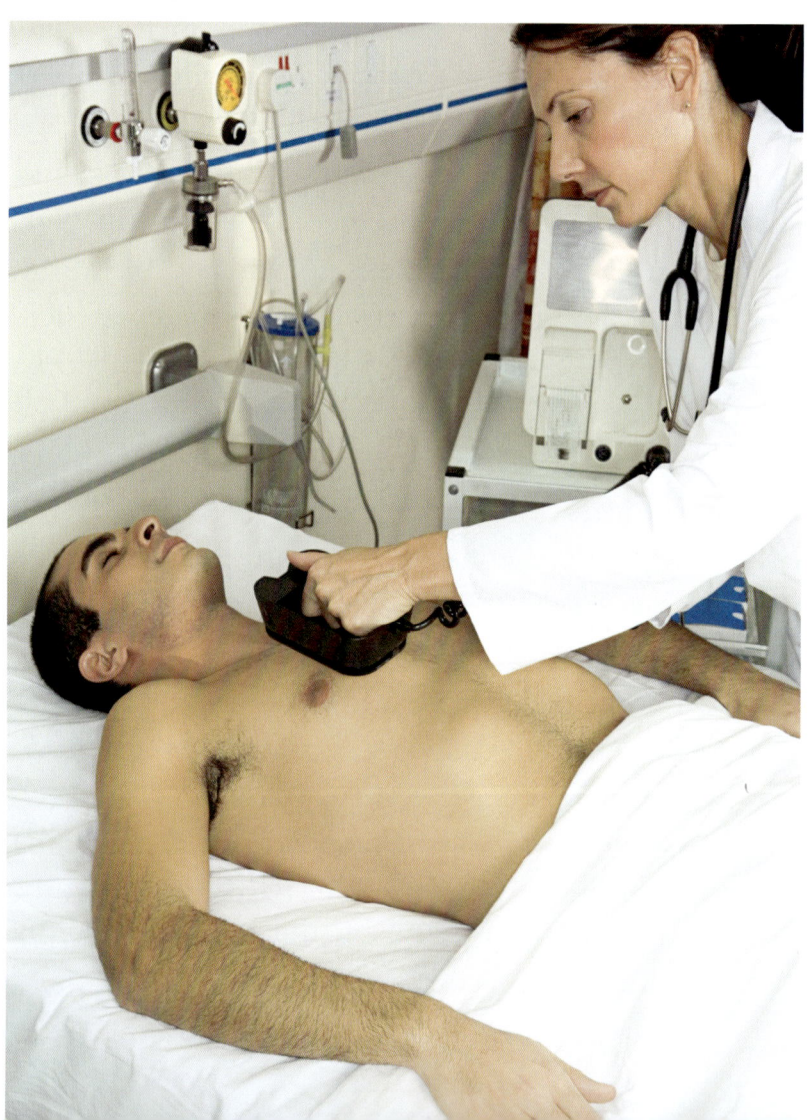

seem to matter. People have died from accidents, illnesses, and during surgery. People are usually considered dead when they stop breathing and their heart stops beating. People who die in hospitals may even be declared dead by doctors before they are brought back. People who have not actually died, but have come very close to death, have also reported having NDEs.

People from all backgrounds and religions have had NDEs. Even **atheists**, people who do not believe in God or an afterlife, have had NDEs. Both adults and children have had NDEs; however, not everyone who dies and then comes back reports having had an NDE.

Bad NDEs

The vast majority of people who have had NDEs consider it to be a positive experience. A few people, however, have had what NDE researcher Dr. Barbara Rommer calls "less than positive" NDEs. These people report having terrifying or painful experiences. They may have had overwhelming feelings of sadness or felt completely alone. They may believe that they had met the devil or had experienced hell.

A policeman named Joseph had a bad NDE after he was hit by a car. During his NDE everything looked gray and black. He saw a figure in a hooded robe and heard people screaming. He saw a hunched-over figure dressed in strips of cloth like a mummy. The figure was shaking. "The screaming

Sometimes people experience bad NDEs and find themselves surrounded by horrible robed figures and terrible screaming.

was horrible," says Joseph. "I couldn't tell if it was coming from that thing or all over the place."[2]

A Life-Changing Experience

Many people who have had NDEs say that the experience changed their lives. Most are no longer afraid of death. They have a greater appreciation for life and for all the good things that they have.

Many people say that the most important thing they learned was that love is the only thing that matters. They may stop caring so much about material things such as houses, cars, and clothes, and instead they may focus more on God, relationships, and helping people. Some people change their lives completely, leaving prestigious and high-paying jobs to become ministers or to help the sick or the poor. No matter how they choose to live the rest of their lives,

Some people find that they have psychic abilities after having an NDE.

> **Visual Test**
>
> **Some researchers have placed signs or computer screens displaying animations in emergency rooms and operating rooms. These displays are placed in such a way that only someone who was floating near the ceiling would be able to see them. No one who has reported having an NDE in these places has seen these displays, suggesting that NDEs may not be real.**

most people who have had an NDE report feeling happier and more fulfilled than they were before their near-death experience.

In addition to feeling more fulfilled, some people who have NDEs report that they have changed in other ways, too. Some people claim to have developed **psychic abilities** due to their NDEs. Others claim that they have been given special knowledge about God and the universe. Still others find that they can no longer wear watches because the watches do not work when they have them on. Or they find that computers and cell phones tend not to work right when they are around them.

Chapter 2

Children and Near-Death Experiences

The NDEs of children are of special interest to researchers because often the children are too young to really understand what death is. In addition, they may not have developed cultural and religious beliefs about what death involves. For example, a small child might not have had time to develop a belief in heaven or hell. In addition, because most young children do not understand that death is permanent, they may not be afraid of death, as many adults are. Another interesting thing about the NDEs of children is that they sometimes report having seen dead relatives that they have never met in life or even heard of. For example, a child might meet a grandparent who had died before the child was born.

Guided by Elizabeth

When she was nine years old, Katie nearly drowned in a swimming pool in a small town in Idaho. She was brought to the emergency room and was not expected to live.

Katie remembers being in the water and feeling very heavy. Then she was in a dark tunnel. She couldn't walk and she was scared. But then a tall, yellow-haired woman appeared and the tunnel got bright. The woman's name was Elizabeth, and she helped Katie. Together they went to heaven. "Heaven was fun!" said Katie. "It was bright and

A child describes to a doctor her drawing of what she saw during her near-death experience.

there were lots of flowers."[3] Katie met many people, including her own grandfather who had died two years before. She also spent time playing with two boys, Mark and Andy, who were souls waiting to be reborn. Finally she met God and Jesus. They asked her if she wanted to see her mother again, and when she said yes, she was returned to her body.

During her NDE, Katie was also able to see what was happening to her body. When she awoke after three days in a **coma**, she was able to exactly describe the emergency room and what the doctors had done to her.

"I Didn't Want to Go Back"

Eleven-year-old Jason also met a lot of people during his NDE. He was hit by a car while riding his bike. He doesn't remember being hit, but he does remember floating about 5 feet (1.5m) above his body. He saw his bloody body and people all around trying to help. Then the ambulance came. Jason tried to tell the people that he was okay, but no one could hear him. Even though they could not hear him, he could hear what the people were saying. He heard someone say that he was dead. Once he knew that he was dead he found himself in a tunnel with a bright light at the end.

Jason traveled upward through the tunnel. When he got to the light he met a lot of people there. They told him that he had to go back because it wasn't his time to die yet. According to Jason, the people did not talk and neither did he. Instead, everyone just understood each other's thoughts. Jason felt like he was in the light for a long time. He felt happy in the light. He felt that everyone loved him there. "When I got to the light I didn't want to go back," he says. "I almost forgot about my body."[4]

Jason traveled back through the tunnel and saw his own body on a table in the hospital. Two doctors were calling his name while trying to save him. Jason woke up in his body. Later, when Jason told his story to the doctor who interviewed him, he said that he was not afraid of death. He told the doctor about a classmate who had recently died of **leukemia**. He said that his friend's death does not make him sad because he knows his friend is in the light.

Some people awake after their near-death experience to find that the doctors are still working to save them.

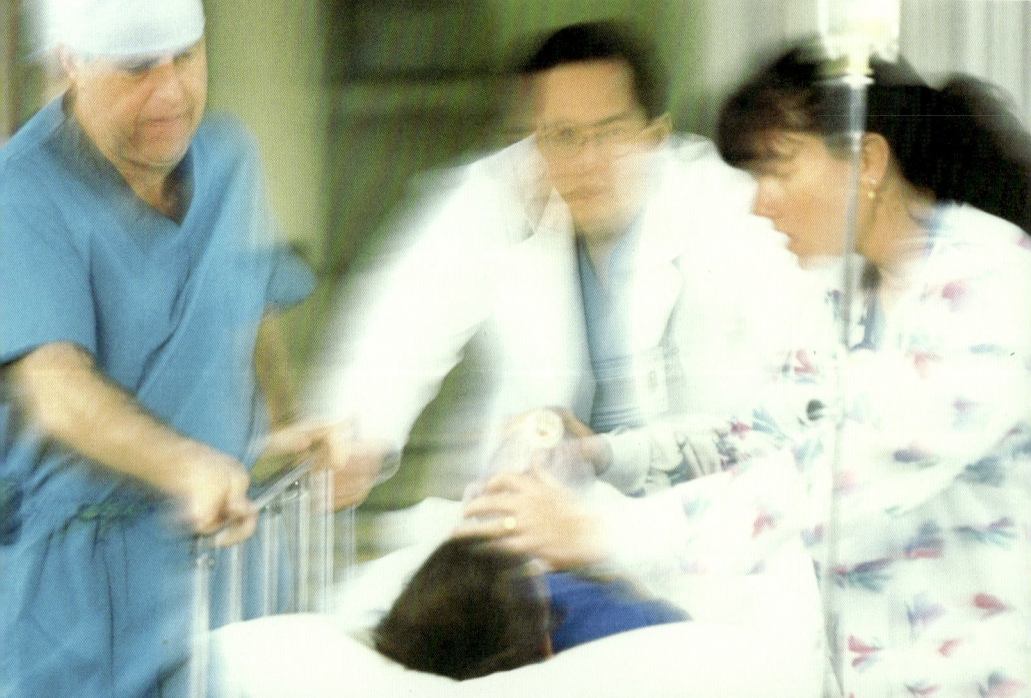

Out-of-Body Experience

The sensation of leaving the body is not restricted to NDEs. It can come from other experiences as well. An epileptic may have a similar sensation during a seizure, and some people have reported having out-of-body experiences while suffering from migraine headaches.

Coming Home

Barbara Springer's experience of heaven was one of great love. When Barbara was twelve years old she died of **scarlet fever**. After she died, she felt herself leaving her body and going into space. Even though everything was black, she did not feel afraid. Then she saw a light and started to move toward it. She moved in a way that is not possible on Earth. "I obviously wasn't walking or skipping or crawling. I was not floating. I was flowing. I was flowing toward the light,"[5] says Barbara.

When she got to the light, it was brighter than anything she had ever seen before, but it did not hurt her eyes. She was sure she was in heaven. Soon, she encountered a heavenly being that radiated light. The being embraced her. "When he embraced me, I could feel the most powerful love," says Barbara. "It

Sometimes people say that they can float during an NDE. They often find themselves floating towards a light and into what they believe is heaven.

is the greatest love that there is in the universe. . . . I felt the love surrounding me. I felt it flowing through me."[6] Barbara felt that the being was God and that she had come home.

Cities of Heaven

Cecil Hamilton also went to heaven, but rather than feeling great love, he received great knowledge. When he was eleven years old he was swimming in a river in Virginia with his brother. His brother started to drown and Cecil tried to save him. But his brother panicked and pulled him under the water. Cecil also began drowning.

Cecil felt peaceful as his spirit rose out of his body. He found himself in a black, empty space with only a speck of light ahead. He traveled quickly toward the light, and when he got there he found that everything seemed to radiate light. There was a river, and on the other side he could see a city. Beyond that city, there was another, and then another. Cecil somehow understood that the first city was "like first grade. People stayed there until they were ready to go to the next city—your eternal progression from city to city."[7]

At the city were three men that Cecil felt were there to welcome and escort him across the river. According to Cecil, "I had the feeling that if I went with them, there would be no coming back, so I hesitated."[8]

Just a Lack of Oxygen

Some scientists believe that a lack of oxygen in the brain may be the cause of people experiencing the dark tunnel with the bright light at the end during NDE experiences. They believe that as a person's eyes get less and less oxygen, the person's eyesight may slowly disappear, starting from the outside edge of the person's line of sight inward toward the center. This might cause the person to believe he or she sees a dark tunnel with a bright light in the center.

Cecil then felt another presence, or being, behind him. This being communicated with him by **telepathy** (tel-EP-uh-thi) and asked him why he had hesitated. Cecil told the being that he was too young to die and that there were some things he wanted to know.

The being allowed Cecil to ask questions. Cecil asked what death was. He was shown a bad car accident in which several people had died. Some of their spirits were rising out of their bodies, but some were not. The being told Cecil that some of the souls might never be reached by God because they did not believe in anything. When Cecil asked how he could tell the difference between right and wrong, the being replied, "Right is helping and being kind. Wrong is not only hurting someone, but not helping when you can." [9]

The being told Cecil many more things, but he also told him that he would not remember most of them. Again, Cecil was given the choice to stay or go back. Cecil wanted to go back to help his mother with his brothers and sisters. The being told Cecil to live in such a way that he would not feel bad when he came back to this place. Cecil awoke back in his body at the bottom of the river. He felt himself being lifted to the surface. After throwing up huge amounts of river water, he found out that his brother had drowned.

During a near-death experience people often find themselves in a tunnel with a bright light just ahead.

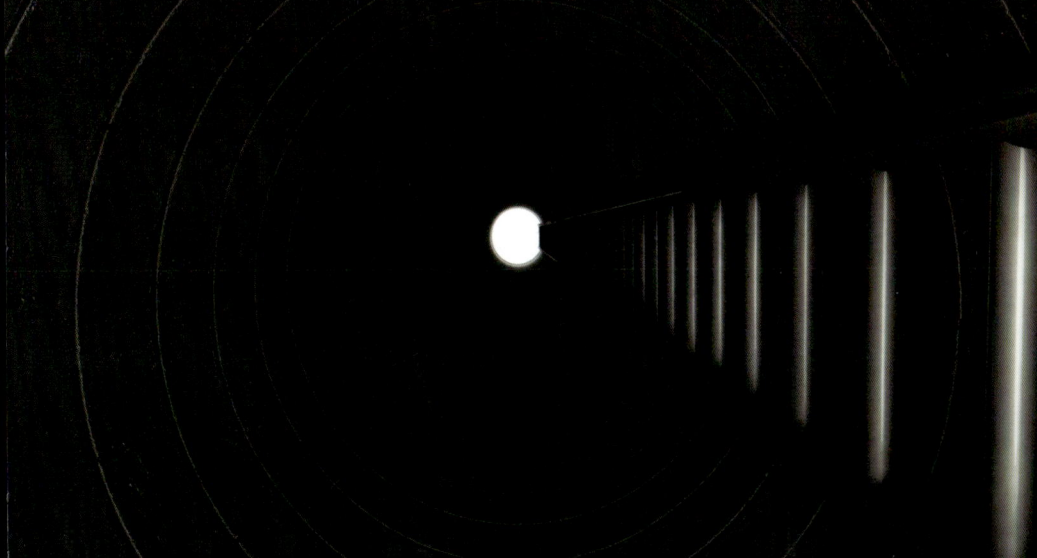

Chapter 3

Accidents and Near-Death Experiences

Sometimes people have an NDE because they were involved in an accident. They may die or come very close to death and then be brought back to life later. Often these people report leaving their bodies and observing the scene of the accident. Usually they are not disturbed to see their own bloody and mutilated bodies. Often they want to reassure the panicked people around their bodies that they are all right, but although they can hear what those people are saying, the still-living people cannot hear or see the spirit of the person who has died.

"I Felt Free"

Lynn Pielage-Kissel had her NDE on June 21, 1976. She was roller skating when she lost control and crashed headfirst into a cement wall. She remembers lying facedown on the roller rink floor in a pool of her own blood. Pielage-Kissel says that she knew that she was going to die. She felt her heart beat for the last time, and as she exhaled for the last time, she felt relaxed and at peace.

Pielage-Kissel felt herself leave her body and says, "Like a cork pulled out of a bottle, I just ran out of my body like liquid."[10] She saw her body on the ground but it did not upset her. Now that she was free of her body she realized how confining it was.

Although they are often at peace during their NDEs, most parents return to their bodies after thinking of their children.

Fear of Dying

Some researchers believe that NDEs are just the brain's attempt to create a positive experience at the time of death so that the person will not be afraid. By giving the person a positive image of the afterlife, the brain controls the person's fear of dying.

Her body was heavy and slow, but now her brain could interpret things like sound and light without the use of her ears and eyes first. For the first time in her life, she felt free. She saw bright colors and heard amazing sounds. According to Pielage-Kissel:

> I wanted to see everything, hear everything, touch everything. I wanted to drink it in as fast as I could. A new beginning was unfolding before me. It seemed as though everything in the universe was right there before me and I was no longer hindered in anyway from experiencing it all firsthand, without a single limitation, . . . I felt so good.[11]

Pielage-Kissel thought she might have stayed like that forever, but then she thought for a moment about her two young daughters that she was leaving behind. Instantly, she was sucked back into her body. When she awoke she was struggling to breathe. She was rushed to the hospital, where she spent several weeks recovering.

Heavenly City

Linda Allen had her NDE after a bicycle accident in Seattle. After the crash she felt herself leaving her body. She panicked because she knew she would not be coming back and she wanted her eight-year-old son to know that there would be someone there to take care of him.

Soon she was rising into the sky, which she describes as being very loving and warm. Four men

Leaving one's body is one of the most common feelings of a near-death experience.

appeared, all wearing worn jeans and plaid shirts. One of the men told her that it was not her time to go yet. The man led her through a life review. Then there were hundreds of spirits all around, she says, "as though they were having a party and they knew me and I knew them. And we were so happy to be there."[12] Allen felt sure that this was not the first time they had all been together.

Allen was then shown a big, beautiful city. "It had golden colors and there was this big explosion coming up over the city of lights and rainbows and colors that we don't have here, that we can't even explain,"[13] says Allen.

An Unpleasant Life Review

Dannion Brinkley also felt love from the being he met in his NDE. Brinkley was talking on the phone in South Carolina in 1975 when a bolt of lightning hit the telephone wire. Thousands of volts of electricity traveled through the line and into Brinkley's head and body. He felt immense pain as the electricity threw him literally out of his shoes and into the air. His heart stopped and his NDE began.

Brinkley found himself in a dark tunnel, traveling toward the light. When he got there he encountered a being of light. "Looking at this Being I had the feeling that no one could love me better, no one could have more empathy, sympathy, encouragement, and nonjudgmental compassion for me than this Being," Brinkley says.[14]

Religious Beliefs

Often people who have NDEs see things during the experience that are consistent with their religious beliefs. For example, Christians are more likely to encounter Jesus, while Muslims are more likely to encounter Muhammad, and Jews, to see Moses.

The being of light engulfed Brinkley, and Brinkley had a life review in which he saw and felt everything that had ever happened to him. He also felt the pain that he had inflicted on other people, and there was a lot of it. According to Brinkley, "I was faced with the sickening reality that I had been an unpleasant person, someone who was self-centered and mean."[15]

Brinkley had been an angry child. His parents could not control him. He teased other children and got into literally thousands of fights. During his life review, Brinkley not only felt his own feelings but also those of the people he had hurt. He felt the humiliation he had caused other children and the frustration and sadness he had caused his parents.

When he had grown up, Brinkley had fought in the Vietnam War. He had killed many enemy soldiers. Although he had not been sorry at the time,

Accidents and Near-Death Experiences

It is not uncommon for people who have had near-death experiences to wake up in the morgue.

during his life review he not only felt the sadness and confusion of the people that he had killed but also the sadness of their grieving loved ones.

Brinkley felt a deep sense of sorrow at the life he had lived. He expected judgment from the being of light, but there was none. The being touched Brinkley, filling him with love and joy. He felt that the burden of guilt had been removed and that he could change his life. The being told him: "Humans are powerful spiritual beings meant to create good on the earth. This good isn't usually accomplished in bold actions, but in singular acts of kindness

The Afterlife

between people. It's the little things that count, because they are more spontaneous and show who you truly are."[16]

When he returned to his body Brinkley found himself in the hospital **morgue**. He had been dead for twenty-eight minutes. Since his NDE, Brinkley claims to have psychic abilities. For example, he no longer plays cards because he can see what cards the other players are holding. Today, Brinkley gives speeches about his experience and volunteers at a **hospice**, comforting those who are dying.

Death on the Battlefield

Like Brinkley, this next story is also about a man who fought in the Vietnam War. This man had his NDE when he was wounded in battle. He had fallen facedown in the mud and was suffocating when he felt himself rise out of his body. He could see his bloody body, but he was not concerned about himself, though he was concerned about his family and hoped they would not see him this way.

Then the soldier saw two other soldiers that he knew. They were also out of their bodies and were starting to walk away. "They motioned for me to come with them but I felt sad for my mother and felt that I couldn't leave my body," says the soldier. "They nodded to me. They seemed to know how I felt and they simply waved good-bye."[17]

The soldier looked down at his body and saw a medic turn his head so that his face was no longer in the mud. The next moment he was back in his body and breathing again.

When he recovered, the soldier spent a great deal of time trying to understand what had happened to him. He eventually talked to Dr. Melvin Morse, an NDE expert. After advising him to learn from his experience, Dr. Morse noticed that the man was not wearing a watch. When he asked about it, the man replied that he did not wear one because "they never work right for me. They always just quit running."[18]

Many near-death experiences occur on the battlefield during war.

Chapter 4

Medicine and Near-Death Experiences

Often NDEs happen as a result of a medical emergency. A person may die during a heart attack or something may go wrong during surgery. Because these patients are often being monitored by medical equipment, the doctors and nurses know exactly when their hearts stopped and when they started up again. Sometimes the patients are even declared dead and then come back to life.

Protected by Loved Ones

Jessica Jaramillo was rushed into emergency surgery. She was bleeding from a carelessly performed **tonsillectomy** that she had had the week before. On the

During an NDE some people may encounter dead relatives that they have never met before, such as grandparents.

way to the operating room, Jaramillo saw her father, who had died when she was just two years old. Her father was surrounded by golden light. He comforted her by rubbing her back and telling her that he loved her and that everything would be okay.

When she was being given **anesthesia**, she saw several of her dead relatives, including great-grandparents that she had never met. She also saw a tall man in a white robe who had eyes that were like rainbows. Jaramillo felt that the man was Jesus. Everyone seemed to glow with a golden light. They all stood in front of the doctors holding hands and praying while the surgery was being performed. By this time, Jaramillo was completely unconscious from the anesthesia. She was comforted by their presence. "I felt so happy and safe to see them all there. I was not scared anymore. I knew everything was going to be okay."[19] When she awoke after the surgery, the people were gone, but Jaramillo is sure that they kept her safe during the emergency surgery that saved her life.

Keeping His Promise

Chris Taylor, a police inspector, also had his NDE during emergency surgery. In November 2001 something went terribly wrong with his **aorta**. He had an extremely painful attack that was witnessed by his son. His son was scared and crying. He asked his father to promise that he would not die. Taylor promised.

Taylor was in surgery for more than ten hours while doctors tried to repair damage caused by a condition that is usually fatal. During this time, a machine was making his heart beat. At the end of the surgery, his heart would not start beating on its own, and the doctor massaged it for 26 minutes in an attempt to save his patient. During the surgery, Taylor felt himself leave his body. He was in a thick gray fog, heading toward a bright light. As he

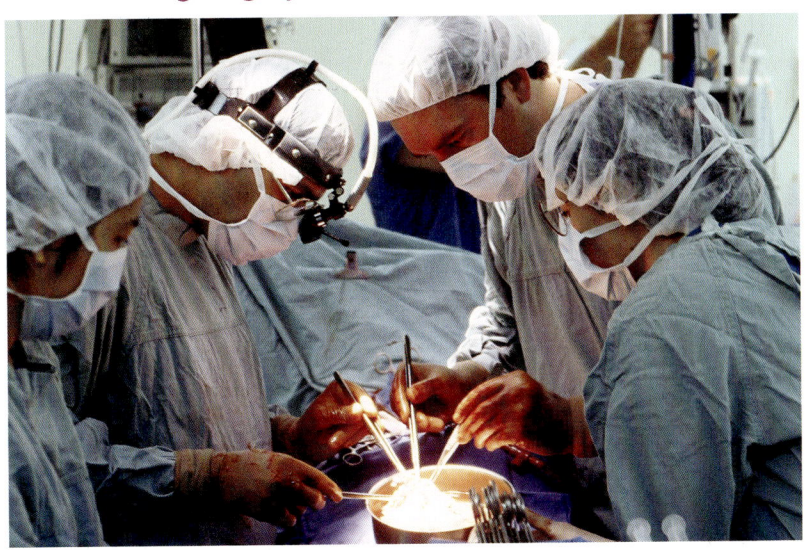

Deaths during surgery have resulted in NDEs.

The Dying Brain

Some researchers believe that NDEs are actually caused by chemicals in the brain. At the time of death, they say, the brain releases a massive dose of chemicals that cause pleasant feelings. This may be why so many people who have NDEs report feeling happy, peaceful, and loved.

approached the light he felt pure love. He also heard voices welcoming him. Even though he felt peaceful he was aware that he was leaving his wife and son behind.

He then saw his wife and son in the waiting room. His son was sobbing and his wife was trying to comfort the boy. When she told him that his father was strong and he should not be afraid, Taylor's son said, "I'm not scared of Dad dying. I know he will not die. He promised me and DAD ALWAYS KEEPS HIS PROMISES."[20] The next moment Taylor was back in his body.

Coffee with Grandma

Jamie also had his NDE in a hospital. His heart stopped for five minutes during surgery when the doctor was inserting a tube into his throat. Jamie's

During an NDE, people may find that they are performing an activity that they did when they were alive, such as having a meal with a loved one.

NDE started when he felt himself floating through a dark tunnel toward a small speck of light. Jamie felt like he was in the tunnel for a long time.

At some point Jamie thought of his grandma who had died three years earlier. Then instantly he was in the light and his grandma was there. She looked about 30 years old. Jamie's grandma invited him to have coffee with her. This was something they had done often when she was alive. Jamie soon noticed that his grandma's table and chairs were there with them. Jamie also noticed that the coffee did not have any taste and although it steamed, it was only lukewarm.

Jamie talked with his grandma, and she told him that she knew that Jamie and his family missed her and that she loved them all. After a while Jamie's grandma told him, "You have to go, you can't stay here, it's not your time."[21] Jamie was upset and begged his grandma to let him stay with her. His grandma reassured him, "You will be back here when it's your time, don't worry."[22] Jamie was still pleading with his grandma to stay when he heard a loud pop and found himself back in his body in the hospital's intensive care unit.

Back from Heaven

Like Jamie, Mary Dooley's NDE resulted from a surgery that did not go right. Dooley was 34 years old and was having a cancerous tumor removed. During her NDE, Dooley left her body and floated through a tunnel toward a bright light. Dooley remembers feeling concerned because she did not have her sunglasses with her, but the light did not hurt her eyes once she got there. Instead, she found the light to be soothing.

Soon Dooley began to notice bright colors; "every color of the rainbow, plus colors I had not ever seen before!"[23] she says. She saw beautiful flowers and grasses. She felt the presence of God all around her and felt that the light was God.

Off to one side, Dooley saw a low wall that was covered with gems of all colors. There was a gate in the wall that was also covered with gems. On the other side of the wall there were heavenly beings. She did not recognize any of them but could feel their love for her. They communicated telepathically with her. The beings asked her if she wanted to stay.

Many people who have had near-death experiences describe heaven as a beautiful place filled with fields of flowers.

Dooley wanted to stay but felt that she had things to do with her life, so she chose to go back. The next moment, she was back in her body.

Dooley is no longer afraid of death. She believes that when she dies she will return to the place in her NDE and go through the gate. "I was in Heaven," says Dooley. "But you have to go through the gate to get to the fun part."[24]

Hope and Love

NDEs like Mary Dooley's are a source of hope for many people. Most people do not want to believe that life is over when the body dies. The fact that most of the people who have had NDEs felt overwhelming feelings of love and peace is comforting to people who have lost loved ones.

NDEs can change not only the lives of those who have them but also the lives of those who hear or read about the experiences. Many people have become kinder and more loving because they have heard about someone else's NDE. According to near-death experiencer Laurelynn Martin, "The only thing we take with us is the love we have given away."[25]

Medicine and Near-Death Experiences

Notes

Chapter One: The Near-Death Experience

1. Quoted in Raymond A. Moody, Jr., *Life After Life*. New York: HarperCollins, 1975, p. 15.
2. Quoted in Barbara A. Rommer, *Blessing in Disguise*. St. Paul, MN: Llewellyn Publications, 2000, p. 62.

Chapter Two: Children and Near-Death Experiences

3. Quoted in Raymond Moody Jr., *The Light Beyond*. New York: Bantam Books, 1988, p. 54.
4. Quoted in Moody, *Life After Life*, Collins, p. 50.
5. Barbara Springer, *Forum of Near-Death Experiences*. (www.near-death.com/forum/nde/000/01.html).
6. Springer, *Forum of Near-Death Experiences*
7. Quoted in P.M.H. Atwater, *The New Children and Near Death Experiences*. Rochester, VT: Bear & Company, 2003, p. 46.
8. Quoted in Atwater, *The New Children and Near Death Experiences*, p. 46.
9. Quoted in Atwater, *The New Children and Near Death Experiences*, p. 46.

Chapter Three:
Accidents and Near-Death Experiences

10. Quoted in Phillip A. Berman, *The Journey Home*. New York: Pocket Books, 1996, p. 39.
11. Quoted in Berman, *The Journey Home*, p. 40.
12. Quoted in Mally Cox-Chapman, *The Case for Heaven*. New York: G.P. Putnam's Sons, 1995, p. 26.
13. Quoted in Cox-Chapman, *The Case for Heaven*, p. 26.
14. Quoted in Lee W. Bailey and Jenny Yates, *The Near Death Experience: A Reader*. New York: Routledge, 1996, p. 64.
15. Quoted in Bailey and Yates, *The Near Death Experience*, p. 64.
16. Quoted in Bailey and Yates, *The Near Death Experience*, pp. 64–70.
17. Melvin Morse, *Transformed by the Light*. New York: Villard Books, 1992, p. 130
18. Melvin Morse, *Transformed by the Light*. p. 130

Chapter Four:
Medicine and Near-Death Experiences

19. Jessica Jaramillo, *Forum of Near-Death Experiences*. (www.near-death.com/forum/nde/000/60.html).
20. Chris Taylor, *Forum of Near-Death Experiences*. (www.near-death.com/forum/nde/000/60.html).
21. Jamie G., Near Death Experience Research Foundation. (www.nderf.org/jaime_g's_nde.htm).
22. Jamie G., Near Death Experience Research Foundation.
23. Quoted in Cox-Chapman, *The Case for Heaven*, p. 15.
24. Quoted in Cox-Chapman, *The Case for Heaven*, p. 16.
25. Quoted in Cox-Chapman, *The Case for Heaven*, p. 48.

Glossary

anesthesia: Drug given by a doctor so that the patient will not feel pain.

aorta: The main artery that carries blood from the heart to the rest of the body.

atheists: People who do not believe in God.

coma: A state of prolonged, deep unconsciousness, usually caused by injury or illness.

hospice: A place or program designed to care for people who are dying.

leukemia: A usually fatal form of cancer in which the body produces too many white blood cells.

life review: The process of seeing and examining one's entire life during a near-death experience.

morgue: A place where dead bodies are kept until they are buried or cremated.

near-death experience (NDE): A vision of the afterlife seen by a person who has come very close to death.

psychic abilities: The ability to know or sense things that cannot be explained by science, such as predicting the future or reading other people's thoughts.

reincarnation: The belief that after a person dies, his or her soul is reborn into a new body.

scarlet fever: A bacterial infection that causes a high fever and red rash and is especially common in children.

soul: The spiritual part of a person that some people believe survives after death.

telepathy (tel-EP-uh-thi): Direct communication from one mind to another without using speech, writing, or signs.

tonsillectomy: Surgery to remove the tonsils, glands in the throat that often become swollen in children.

For Further Exploration

Books:

Janet Lee Carey, *Wenny has Wings.* New York: Atheneum, 2004. This award-winning middle-grade novel is about eleven-year-old Will who is nearly killed in an auto accident that does kill his younger sister. In the hospital, Will has an NDE in which he sees his sister in the light. The book is written as a series of letters from Will to his sister.

Elaine Landau, *Mysteries of Science: Near Death Experiences.* Brookfield, CT: Millbrook Press, 1996. Informational book about NDEs.

Michael Martin, *Near-Death Experiences.* Mankato, MN: Capstone Press, 2005. This book provides information about NDEs, including the history of NDEs, scientific investigations, common elements of NDEs, and interesting facts.

Jan Thornhill, *I Found a Dead Bird: The Kids' Guide to the Cycle of Life and Death.* Toronto: Maple Tree Press, 2006. This colorful, informative book investigates death in both people and nature. Includes a wealth of interesting sidebars, charts, and photos.

Web Sites:

Into the Light (www.melvinmorse.com/images.htm). This Web site has several pictures drawn by children who have had NDEs. Includes explanations by NDE expert Dr. Melvin Morse.

Near-Death Experiences and the Afterlife (www.near-death.com/index.html). Extensive Web site that includes many stories from people who have had NDEs, information from NDE experts, and a frequently-asked-questions section.

NDERF: Near Death Experience Research Foundation (www.nderf.org/). A huge Web site where users can read about other people's NDEs and post their own stories. Also includes articles and book excerpts.

Index

accidents and NDE
  examples of, 25–31
  overview, 24
Allen, Linda, 27–28
anesthesia, 34
aorta, 35
atheists, 11

barriers, 9
battlefield experiences, 31–32
beings
  choice of return to life and, 23
  dead relatives, 15–16, 17, 34, 37–38
  as escorts, 21–23
  heaven and, 15–16, 19, 21
  knowledge and, 21–23
  life review and, 28–31
  meeting as commonality of NDE, 9
  negative NDEs and, 11
  telepathic communication and, 18, 22
brain
  dying and, 26, 36
  oxygen deprivation and, 22
Brinkley, Dannion, 28–31
Buddhism, 4

children and NDE
  coma and, 17
  dead relatives and, 15–17
  examples of, 16–23
  fear of death and, 15
  leukemia and, 18
  out-of-body experiences, 16–19
  overview, 15–16
  research on, 15
  scarlet fever, 19

choice to return to life, *See* return to life
Christianity, 4, 29
colors, 26, 28, 34, 38
coma, 17
computers, 14

dead relatives, 15–16, 17, 34, 37–38
devil, 11
Dooley, Mary, 38–39
drowning, 16, 21–23
drugs, 6

epilepsy, 19

fear of death, 15
floating. *See* out-of-body experience
freedom, 25–27

Hamilton, Cecil, 21–23
heaven, 4, 15–17, 20–21
hell, 4, 11, 15
Hinduism, 4
hospice, 31

Islam, 4, 29

Jaramillo, Jessica, 33–34
Jesus, 17, 29, 34
Judaism, 29

ketamine, 6
knowledge, 14, 21–23

leukemia, 18
life-changing experience, 12–14, 39
life review, 9, 28–31

light, 8–9, 17–20, 28–29, 34–35, 37–38
lightning, 28
love, 9, 13, 19, 21, 27–28, 30, 36, 39

Martin, Laurelynn, 39
medicine and NDE
  aorta, 35
  anesthesia, 34
  dying brain, 36
  overview, 33
  surgery and, 33–39
  tonsillectomy, 33
migraine headache, 19
morgue, 30, 31
Morse, Melvin, 32
Moses, 29
Muhammad, 29

near-death experience (NDE)
  barriers and, 9
  coma and, 17
  definition, 6–7
  description of, 5, 7, 7–10
  drugs and, 6
  as life-changing experience, 12–14, 39
  negative experiences, 11–12, 12
  religious beliefs and, 4, 6, 11, 29
  return to life, 9–10, 18, 23, 26–28, 31, 35–36, 39
  surgery and, 10, 33–39, 35
  See also accidents and NDE; children and NDE; medicine and NDE
negative NDE, 11–12, 12

out-of-body experience
  children and, 16–19, 21–23
  as commonality of NDE, 8, 27
  epileptic experience and, 19
  freedom sensation and, 25
  illustration of, 7
  inability to leave, 31
  life review and, 9, 27–28
  migraine headaches and, 19
  observance of self and, 8, 17, 24, 25, 31
  surgery and, 35–39
  telepathy and, 26
oxygen deprivation, 22

Pielage-Kissel, Lynn, 25–27
psychic abilities and experiences, 13, 14, 18, 22, 26, 31,

rainbows, 28, 34, 38
reincarnation, 6
relatives, 9, 15–16, 34, 36–38
religious beliefs, 4, 6, 11, 29
research, 14–16
return to life
  barriers and, 9
  children and, 17–18, 23, 26–27, 35–36
  command to return, 9–10, 17
  own choice, 23, 39
  reasons for, 26–27, 31, 35–36
Rommer, Barbara, 11

sadness, 11, 30
scarlet fever, 19
soul, 4
Springer, Barbara, 19–21
surgery, 11, 33–39

Taylor, Chris, 35–36
telepathy, 18, 22, 26, 38
  See also psychic abilities and experiences
tonsillectomy, 33
tunnel
  as commonality of NDE, 8
  heaven and, 16
  light and, 16–18, 23, 28, 37, 38

Vietnam War, 29, 31

war, 31–32, 32
watches, 14, 31

Picture Credits

Cover: photos.com
© Adamsmith/Taxi/Getty Images, 18
© Altrendo Images/Altrendo/Getty Images, 13
AP Images, 32
© David Buffington/Blend Images/Getty Images, 37
© Rich Frishman/Time Life Pictures/Getty Images, 16
© Michael Gesinger/Photonica/Getty Images, 27
© Headhunters/Photographer's Choice RF/Getty Images, 12
© Historical Picture Archive/Corbis, 7
Robert J. Huffman. Field Mark Publications. Reproduced by permission. 25
© Image Source Pink/Image Source/Getty Images, 10
© Images.com/Corbis, 5
© Jupiterimages, 20, 34
© Shuji Kobayashi/Stone/Getty Images, 30
© Riko Pictures/Photographer's Choice RF/Getty Images, 23
© Louie Psihoyos/Science Faction/Getty Images, 35
© Pete Turner/Riser/Getty Images, 39

About the Author

Rachel Lynette has written more than twenty books for children as well as many articles on children and family life. She also teaches science to children of all ages. Rachel lives in the Seattle area in the Songaia Cohousing Community with her two children, David and Lucy, a cat named Cosette, and a playful rat. When she isn't teaching or writing, she enjoys spending time with her family and friends, traveling, reading, drawing, crocheting hats and socks, and inline skating.

Wake Tech. Libraries
9101 Fayetteville Road
Raleigh, North Carolina 27603-5696

WAKE TECHNICAL COMMUNITY COLLEGE
3 3063 00140220 4

WN DATE DUE

DEC 0 2 2008			
12/19/08			
FEB 2 2 2009			

GAYLORD — PRINTED IN U.S.A.

MAR '07